KARATE

Junior Sports

Morgan Hughes

Rourke
Publishing LLC
Vero Beach, Florida 32964

www.rourkepublishing.com

PHOTO CREDITS: Cover Yvonne Hemsey/Getty; p 5, 18 Matthew Stockman/Getty; p 6, 25 Chung Sung-Jun/Getty; title page, p 9, 11, 15, 16, 20, 22, 23 Photos.com; p 12 Robert Nickelsberg/Getty; p 13 Bob Nichols/Getty; p 19 Jed Jacobsohnn/Getty; p 26 Markus Boesch/Getty; p 27 Simon Ridgway/Getty; p 29 AFP/Getty

Title page: *One of the most important goals of every student of martial arts is to gain a sense of calm self-confidence.*

Editor: Frank Sloan

Library of Congress Cataloging-in-Publication Data

Hughes, Morgan, 1957-
  Karate / Morgan Hughes.
    p. cm. -- (Junior sports)
  Includes bibliographical references and index.
  ISBN 1-59515-193-1 (hardcover)
  1. Karate--Juvenile literature. I. Title. II. Series: Hughes, Morgan, 1957- Junior sports.
  GV1114.3.H84 2004
  796.815'3--dc22

                              2004009373

Printed in the USA

CG/CG

TABLE OF CONTENTS

WHAT IS KARATE?

The word "karate" is Japanese for "empty hand." Karate began hundreds of years ago among peasants in Japan who were forced to fight their enemies without the use of formal weapons. Instead they developed a form of fighting, using their hands and feet and their elbows and knees.

Karate is a high-energy sport that teaches discipline and self-defense.

There is an important lesson all students of martial arts learn, long before they master any of the punches or kicks. That principle is that the martial arts are about self-defense. Karate is about respect and **restraint**, not beating people up or showing how tough you are.

The most accomplished karate student is the one who will never have to use his or her skills away from the training hall, or *dojo*. It is the goal of every martial artist to walk in peace and harmony, to use the mind and not the fists to solve problems.

Karate helps build both physical and mental skills. In addition to strength, flexibility, self-confidence, and endurance, students typically increase powers of concentration and focus.

The relationship between martial arts student and teacher is built on respect.

THE BOW

Every karate lesson or training session begins and ends with a **courtesy** bow to the instructor, or *sensei*. Among the many "stances" in karate, the bow is one of the most important, for it shows your respect for your teacher. Learning respect is a lesson you can use in everyday life.

While an instructor is known as *sensei*, the head instructor of a group of schools is called a *shihan*.

When performing a traditional bow, either to your instructor or to another student, stand very still and bend only at the waist.

When bowing to your sensei, lean slightly forward and avert your eyes.

STANCES

The two basic categories of stances are offensive and defensive. The defensive stances give you stability, balance, and proper alignment. They enable you to be ready if an opponent strikes. The offensive stances also stress balance and stability, and they prepare you to launch a kick or a punch.

The most basic "ready" stance is the Front Stance. In this stance, place one foot ahead of the other, your body turned slightly. Your weight should be **distributed** so that 60 to 70 percent is on your front leg. Your hands are in a "boxing" stance, fists ready.

Stances are categorized by *tachi*, which refers to the lower part of the body, and *kamae*, which means the upper body.

From the Front Stance, you can do just about anything, from throwing a punch to launching a kick or executing a successful block.

The Horse Stance is named because you begin by positioning your feet wide, as if on horseback. Your feet should be a little more than shoulder width apart. Your knees are more deeply bent than in many stances. Your fists (palm up) should be coiled just above the hips.

The Horse Stance is a basic in any karate class. The longer you can hold it, the better.

The Horse Stance is extremely popular on the training mat. It is commonly used when practicing many different kinds of strikes and punches. Because of its somewhat exaggerated knee bend, the Horse Stance is also excellent for building strength in the legs.

From the Horse Stance, you can throw forward punches or execute strikes to either side.

PUNCHES

One of the most basic strikes in karate is the Straight Punch. To deliver a punch correctly, you must learn how to make a proper fist. Hold your hands in front of you and curl your fingertips tightly toward your palms. Then roll your hands into balls with your thumbs along the front of your fingers.

To deliver a right-hand punch, begin with your right fist, palm up, at your right hip. Your left fist should be palm down, slightly **extended**. The punch begins by pulling your left fist back. At the same time, rotate the right fist into a palm-down position as you extend powerfully forward.

The right (or left) Front Punch is a powerful weapon and can be delivered to the stomach, torso, neck, or face.

In a basic karate punch, the actual striking surface is the row of knuckles along the top of the fist, not the front of the fist.

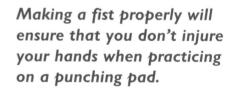

Making a fist properly will ensure that you don't injure your hands when practicing on a punching pad.

STRIKES

Basic strikes include the Elbow Strike and the Back Fist. The most famous strike is what many people think of as the "karate chop." It is actually called Knife Hand or Ridge Hand. It employs the outer edge of the stiffened hand and is most effectively used on a soft target.

Karate is, in many ways, the art of exploding energy. When a kick or punch or strike is delivered, it is common to discharge a loud *kiai*, a shout sometimes referred to as a "spirit yell."

Proper body and foot position allows you to launch any of a number of strikes, using both hands and feet. Keep your front hand high and your back hand coiled to strike. Stay on your toes and maintain your balance so you can shift forward and back, right and left.

The Ready Stance resembles a boxing stance with one difference. Notice how these competitors are on their toes, ready to kick.

The Back Fist is used against an opponent who is standing in front of you. Begin with the striking hand close to the chest. Then, with a quick, snapping motion, extend the fist outward to the target area, knuckles first. The striking hand is quickly brought back to a ready position.

When delivering a Back Fist strike (*uraken*), you are looking for several common targets. These include the bridge of the nose, temple, or cheekbone.

A common target for a Back Fist is the opponent's solar plexus, or chest.

It is very important, when delivering a Front Kick, to bend the toes back toward your body so you don't jam them when you strike with the ball of your foot.

The first kick you'll learn as a karate student is the Front Kick.

KICKS

Three of the main kicks in karate are the Front Kick, the Side Kick, and the Roundhouse Kick. The Front Kick uses the ball of the foot as the weapon. The Side Kick uses the outside edge of the striking foot. The Roundhouse Kick may use the ball or front of the foot.

A Side Kick is delivered from an open stance and relies on a snapping action of the leg. On the other hand, the Roundhouse Kick can begin from either a front or back stance. It requires excellent balance, as you must bring your striking foot behind you at about waist level before extending the kick.

Known as the *mawashi-geri*, the Roundhouse Kick can be used on a low, middle, or high target. It requires great balance and hours of practice, but can be extremely effective.

Notice that the striking point for a Side Kick is the outer edge of the foot.

Even with a very high side kick, the *striking surface* is the *outside edge* of the foot and the heel, not the bottom of the foot.

With practice, you can kick targets higher even than your own head.

BLOCKS

Because karate is the art of self-defense, you must learn to fend off attacks with special blocks. The three most basic blocks are the Low Block (used against kicks), the Middle Block (used against straight punches), and the High Block (used against overhead attacks).

A Low Block may be delivered with an arm or, as in this photo, a leg.

To deliver a Low Block and successfully defend against a kick, you should use a downward sweeping motion. With your fist palm down, extend your forearm to absorb the blow before the kick can reach your body. This can be used either to the left or right side, depending on the attacker.

The Middle Block uses an up-and-outward sweeping motion. Depending on the style of the block, the fist may be turned in or turned out. Either way, your arm ends up in a **vertical** position. Like the Low Block, you can perform this block to the left or right, depending on your attacker.

The outward motion of the Middle Block keeps the attacker's punch from finding its target.

UNIFORMS AND BELTS

The uniform worn on the training mat is called a *gi*. It consists of loose fitting-pants and a wrap-around jacket. The jacket is held closed by a colored belt, or *obi*, which is tied in a special knot. The usual order of belt colors from beginner to expert is white, orange, yellow, blue, green, purple, brown, and black.

The black belt is the most honored symbol of achievement in karate.

There are 10 black belt rankings (or *dans*). According to World Karate Federation requirements, you must be at least 70 years old to earn the highest (10th) degree. This ultimate black belt is called a *Judan*.

Even if you train three hours a week, you may need up to three years before earning a first-degree black belt. There are nine additional degrees after that. For example, a seventh degree black belt can take up to 25 years of training.

Black belt experts can perform all kinds of unbelievable feats of strength.

GLOSSARY

courtesy (KUR tuh see) — polite behavior that shows respect for another person

dojo (DOE joe) — Japanese word for the training hall or studio

distributed (dis TRIB yuht ed) — divided or separated into parts or portions

extended (ek STEND ud) — stretched or pulled out to full length

fend off (FEND OFF) — to defend against or keep at a distance

gi (JEE) — Japanese word for a karate uniform, worn on the practice mat

Judan (JOO dahn) — Japanese word for the highest black belt rank possible (10th degree)

kamae (kah MAY) — Japanese word for the position of the upper part of the body; torso

kiai (kee AAH) — the Japanese "spirit yell" used with punches and kicks for emphasis

mawashi-geri (mah WASH ee GAIR ee) — Japanese word for roundhouse kick

obi (OH bee) — Japanese word for the belt worn by karate students

restraint (reh STRAYNT) — self-control

reversal (ruh VUR suhl) — changing the direction or order of an activity to the opposite of the original

sensei (SENN say) — Japanese word for the teacher or instructor

shihan (SHEE han) — Japanese word for the head instructor for several schools

tachi (ta CHEE) — Japanese word for the position of the lower part of the body

uraken (oo RAH ken) — Japanese word for a backfist strike

vertical (VUR tuh kul) — at right angles to the horizon; pointing upward

Further Reading

Carlon, Roger, and Jane Hallander. *Super Karate for Kids.* Unique Publications, 2000

Dunphy, Michael J., et al. *The Kids' Karate Book.* Workman Publishing Company, 1999

Mitchell, David. *DK Superguide: Martial Arts.* Penguin Books, Ltd, 2000

Morris, Neil. *Get Going: Karate,* Heinemann Library, 2002

Websites to Visit

childrentoday.com/resources/articles/martialarts.htm

karateforkids.tripod.com/

www.kinderstart.com/sportsandexercise/martialarts.html

www.usakarate.org

Index

About the Author

Morgan Hughes is the author of more than 50 books on hockey, track and field, bicycling, and many other subjects. He lives in Connecticut with his wife, daughter, and son.